Anitha Bennett has written for children from preschool to preteen levels, and specialises in activity-oriented books. Her previous publications include *My Gourmet Kook Book, Treasures from Trash, Alphabet Activities, This and That, Paper Craft* and *The Complete Science Activity Book*.

Anitha lives in Chennai with her family.

MORE PAPER CRAFT

Anitha Bennett

SCHOLASTIC
New York Toronto London Auckland Sydney
Mexico City New Delhi Hong Kong Buenos Aires

Text and illustrations © 2009 Anitha Bennett

All rights reserved.

Published by Scholastic India Pvt. Ltd.
A subsidiary of Scholastic Inc., New York, 10012 (USA).
Publishers since 1920, with international operations in
Canada, Australia, New Zealand, the United Kingdom,
Mexico, India, Argentina, and Hong Kong.

No part of this publication may be reproduced in whole or
in part, or stored in a retrieval system, or transmitted in any
form or by any means, electronic, mechanical, photocopying,
recording, or otherwise without the written permission of the
publisher.

For information regarding permission, write to:
Scholastic India Pvt. Ltd.
Golf View Corporate Tower-A, 3rd Floor,
DLF Phase V, Gurgaon 122002 (India)

First edition: September 2009

ISBN-10: 81-8477-391-9
ISBN-13: 978-81-8477-391-0

Printed at Parangat Offset, New Delhi

CONTENTS

Craft Box	1
Pop-up Card	4
Doily Bowl	7
Newspaper Scarecrow	10
Playing Cards	13
Room Divider	16
Popcorn Holder	19
Tissue Paper Flowers	22
Paper Skirt	24
Photoframe	27
Memory Cards	29
Greeting Card Curtain	32
Decoupage Box	35
Paper Earrings	38
Paper Jewels	41
Paper Toffees	44
Hoops	47
Magnetic Notepad	49

Shadow Box Display	52
Handprint Paper Stationery	55
Cut-out Cards	58
Personalised Height Chart	61
Placemats	64
Sun-prints	66
Garden Mobile	68
Glass Painting	71
Gift Toppers	74
Drawer Divider	77
Cardboard Bulletin Board	80
Paper Quill Picture	83
Tie and Dye Paper	85
Waxed Paper Postcards	88
Confetti	90
Paper Blocks for 3D Origami	92
Origami Wreath	95
Cake Toppers	98
Art Corner	101
Pocketbook	104
Venetian Mask	107
Point-a-Picture	110

Craft Box

What will you do with all the paper projects that you are going to make from this book? Here's a handy box to store your projects in without messing up your house.

You will need
1 cardboard box
1 sheet of thick cardboard paper
Light coloured gift-wrapping paper
Craft knickknacks (bottle caps, buttons, shells, etc.)
40 ice-cream sticks   Fevicol
Decorative paraphernalia (stickers, sketch pens, paints, etc.)

Here we go
1. Clean the cardboard box and cut off the flaps that make the lid.
2. Stick gift-wrapping paper all around the box. If you have the time (and patience) you can wrap the insides as well.
3. Write MY PAPER CRAFT BOX on one side of the carton with ice-cream sticks and glue. You may have to make the sticks shorter to form certain alphabets.
4. Decorate the rest of the sides with knickknacks and Fevicol. Make a collage on one side if you have scrap cloth. You could also stick buttons along the border.

To make the lid
1. Measure the size (the length and the breadth) of your cardboard box on the top.
2. Add 2" to make the lid. For example, if your box measures 15" x 10", you will have to cut 17" x 12" for the lid.
3. Using a ruler, measure 1.5" from each side of the cut cardboard piece and draw lines along the sides to mark the 1.5" border.

4. Now carefully fold along the lines.
5. Make slits by cutting on the dotted lines.

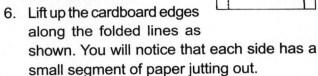

6. Lift up the cardboard edges along the folded lines as shown. You will notice that each side has a small segment of paper jutting out.
7. Stick the edges to their nearest adjacent side to make a neat lid.

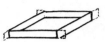

8. Fit the lid on the box and you have a safe locker for all your paper creations!

More to do
- Label your box: (your name)'s CRAFT BANK or come up with your own label to make it completely personal.
- Measure and fit a thick cardboard sheet in the middle of the box to divide it into two. Store your craft supplies on one side and your finished goodies on the other!

Pop-up Card

Have you seen the smart little cards that have pop-up surprises in the middle? Here's a simple card that can be made without too much fuss and that is sure to make the recipient happy.

You will need

1 thick chart paper
Markers/Sketch pens
Scissors
Pencil

Here we go

1. Cut a 12" x 8" rectangular piece from the chart paper. With this measurement, you will get a normal-sized card of 6" x 4".

2. Fold the paper in half to form a card.
3. Draw a line from the folded edge of the card to the centre. CUT →
4. Cut along the line starting at the folded edge.
5. Fold back the top flap to form a triangle and crease with your fingers. Do the same with the bottom flap to form a triangle and crease with your fingers.
6. Now put the flaps back in place.
7. Open up the card like a tent. Using your thumb or fingers, push the triangles into the inside of the card.
8. Close the card and press firmly.
9. Now open it and you have a mouth pop-up!

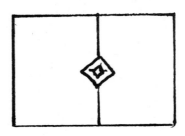

10. Using markers, draw a simple face around the mouth. Add a greeting and your pop-up will talk when you open the card!

More to do
- You can vary the size of the card according to your requirement. Count the number of members in your family and make a tall card. Cut mouth pop-ups of different sizes, one below the other, leaving some gap in between (to draw the faces), so you can have the whole family wish when someone opens the card!
- Try drawing a jagged line instead of a simple straight one and you will have a sharp set of teeth pop-up instead!

Doily Bowl

Have you seen pretty punched out paper doilies decorating a table? Here's a better way to adorn the table with them—in the form of bowls!

You will need
1 pack of paper doilies   1 plastic cling wrap
2 small plastic containers (smaller than the doilies)
1 plate   1 paintbrush
Fevicol

Here we go
1. Take four paper doilies from your doily pack.
2. In a small plate, dilute some Fevicol with a few drops of water till it comes to a consistency with which you can paint freely.

3. Stick the doilies to each other, one below the other, with this mixture. You can stick two at a time. Allow it to dry a little and stick them together. Do not allow the doilies to dry out.
4. Cover the plastic bowl with a layer of cling wrap.
5. Turn the plastic bowl upside down on a newspaper.

6. Coat the back of the bowl over the cling wrap with Fevicol. You may have to add more Fevicol if the glue doesn't stay on the wrap.
7. When your doilies are slightly dry but still malleable, drape them carefully over the bowl.
8. Firmly press down on all sides, to smooth out any wrinkles. If your doily does not drape your entire bowl, then you will have to start out from step 4 again with a smaller bowl.

9. To lock the doily firmly in place, cover another bowl of the same size with cling wrap and invert it over the doily bowl.

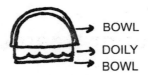

→ BOWL
→ DOILY
→ BOWL

10. Allow the doily bowl to dry for a couple of days.
11. Now carefully remove the top bowl. Dislodge the cling wrap from the bottom bowl and you will have your doilies retaining the shape of the bowl. Fill your doily bowl with candy to make a perfect table centrepiece!

More to do

- Add a few drops of acrylic paint to the Fevicol mixture before coating the back of the bowl. You will have a tinted bowl with a different colour on the side.
- You could even decorate the bowl with sequins, bells and mirrors.

Newspaper Scarecrow

Do you have loads of newspapers piled up in a corner? You can use them to make this fun paper scarecrow for your garden.

You will need

1 thick round paper plate
Piles of newspapers
String/Thread
Glue

1 long stick
Scissors
Coloured paper
Brown tape

Here we go

1. To make the face, turn the paper plate over.
2. Cut out two paper circles for the eyes and stick them on the plate.

3. Cut the shape for the nose. Fold it in half. Now stick it on the plate (stick the shaded region). You will have a pop-up nose.
4. Cut out a big smiley mouth and stick it below the nose.
5. Now tear or cut 2" wide newspaper strips lengthwise.
6. Gather at least 40-50 such strips.
7. Divide the strips into four equal bunches.

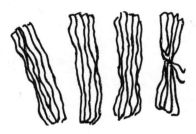

8. Tie a string to the centre of the bunches.
9. To assemble the scarecrow, tape the paper plate to the stick.
10. Tie the first bunch of papers right under the taped face (see the next page).

11. Tie the rest of the bunches either one below the other or around as shown.
12. Plant the stick in your garden for a sunny summer scarecrow!

More to do
- Make smaller scarecrows and use them to label your garden plants. Attach rectangular labels made out of cardboard below the taped faces to write the names of the plants. Then attach the newspapers.
- Make a larger scarecrow. Instead of attaching the newspapers under the paper plate face, tie them above it. You will have a scarecrow with a mop top for your garden!

Playing Cards

With a little bit of effort you can have personalised playing cards that will fit in your hand and that you will never find in a store.

You will need
4 thick chart papers (same colour)
Scissors   Theme-based pictures
Glitter pens, sketch pens and paints
Glue

Here we go
1. Cut a piece from the chart paper the size of a playing card. You can stick to the size of a normal playing card or increase its size all around by an inch for a bigger-sized card.

2. With this sample card as a template, cut out 54 cards (52 cards and two jokers) of the same size, from the chart paper.
3. Figure out a theme for your cards. It can be cars, planes, cartoon faces or anything else.
4. Cut and gather pictures on this theme from magazines and newspapers. You could even find stickers.
5. Paste each of them on one side of the cards.

6. Next, take a pack of actual cards and observe where the numbers and the four shapes are marked.
7. Using sketchpens, mark the cards—all 52 of them. You can mark the King, Queen, Jack and Ace with glitter pens! Joker cards can be left blank or you can doodle on them.

8. Start playing. You are sure to have hours of fun with this pack.

More to do
- Get each of the cards laminated. That will make them last longer. It will also be easier to wipe them clean.
- Gift a pack! If you know what your recipient loves, collect theme-based pictures and stick on the cards and surprise him/her.

Room Divider

MORE PAPER CRAFT

Here is how you can add a picturesque room divider to your room to separate your study area from your bed or just to cordon off a private nook for yourself.

You will need
1 tall cardboard box (a refrigerator box is best)
Scissors   Paints and brushes
Flowerpots (at least six pots to act like a stand)

Here we go
1. Cut all the way through one of the joints of the refrigerator box lengthwise.
2. Now open it and you

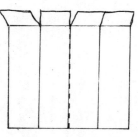

will have one continuous piece of cardboard with four sections and three bends in between.
3. Cut off the lids of the box.
4. Draw and paint natural scenery on one side of the divider. The scenery could include mountains, a river, the sun, clouds and some trees. Make sure your drawings are spaced out between the four sections.
5. Allow this side to dry.
6. Next, paint the other side with a rural scene that can include a well, huts, cows and coconut trees. Let it dry.
7. Now, sandwich the divider between two flower-pots on either side to help it to stand.

8. Your divider is ready to liven up you room.

More to do
- If the space is too small and you can't use flowerpots, stand your divider between two chairs on either side or one chair each at opposite ends.
- It would be great if you could fit a wooden stand or a frame to your cardboard room divider so it can stand independently. Ask your local carpenter for more options.

Popcorn Holder

Wouldn't you love to make a set of popcorn holders that can be used again and again?

You will need
Corrugated paper (the ridged paper inside biscuit boxes)
1 thick chart paper   Pencil
Glue   Scissors
2 metres of broad satin ribbon

Here we go
1. Take a strip of the corrugated paper you get in tin biscuit boxes and glue the ends together.
2. Place this cylinder on the chart paper and draw its outline.

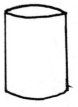

MORE PAPER CRAFT

3. Using a compass, draw another circle, 1" bigger, around the circle drawn in step 2.

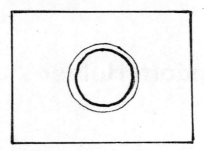

4. Now cut out the bigger circle.
5. Make slanting lines between the inner and outer circle as shown.

6. Cut along the lines to get a fringed circle.
7. Apply glue on the fringes.
8. Now place the corrugated cylinder on the circle. Stick the fringes all around the cylinder as shown.

9. Cut two pieces of satin ribbon to fit the circumference of the container. Paste the satin ribbon around the top and the bottom for a neat finish.

10. Now you can fill your popcorn holder with popcorn and enjoy your snack.

More to do
- To keep the container from soiling, line it with a few pieces of tissue paper before putting in the popcorn.
- You can even use the container to store knickknacks or candy.

Tissue Paper Flowers

Did you know that you can make carnations out of plain tissue paper? Grab a box each of white and pink tissue paper to make yourself a bouquet.

You will need
For 1 flower:
1 piece of wire
3 white tissue papers   3 pink tissue papers

Here we go
1. Stack the tissue papers, alternating the pink with the white.
2. Now carefully fanfold the tissue papers together lengthwise.

3. Gather the folded papers in your hand and fold them in the middle.
4. Twist a wire around the centre to hold the stack together.
5. With the wire pointing downward, slowly and gently open each tissue paper towards the top as shown.
6. Squish and fluff each layer as you peel it to make it look like a flower.
7. Do the same till you pull up all six layers.
8. Your flower is ready. Make a bunch and put it in a vase.

More to do
- Snip off the ends of the tissue with scissors for a more natural look.
- If you have tissues only of a single colour, tint the edges of every alternate tissue in the stack with pastel colours.

Paper Skirt

If you enjoy playing dress up then here is a fun skirt you can make. You can even adapt it as a Hawaiian lei or a tribal chief's outfit!

You will need
Crepe paper streamers   Chart paper
3" Velcro piece   Glue
Fevicol
Tissue paper flowers (refer to previous activity)

Here we go
1. Cut a chart paper strip that is 6" longer than your waist size and about 2" wide. This will be your waistband.
2. Now cut the paper streamers to the length that you want your skirt to be.

3. Use streamers of different colours for a multicoloured skirt. When you have about 50 streamer pieces ready, you can start putting them together.
4. Attach each streamer to one side of your waistband with glue. You can stick the streamers side by side or you can overlap them for a chunkier skirt.
5. Let the skirt dry completely.
6. Attach the Velcro with Fevicol at two ends of the waistband. The soft part on the inner side at one end and the prickly part on the outer side at the other end.

7. Once the Velcro dries, add paper crepe flowers to your skirt and you are ready to sway.

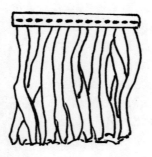

More to do
- Make a short skirt with gold and silver paper strips. Add some glitter and your fairy outfit is ready.
- You can also make a tribal chief's outfit by using a roll of brown paper, painting tiger stripes on it and cutting it up into strips.

Photoframe

A great way to display your favourite photos is to frame them up and hang them around the house or place them on shelves.

You will need

Cardboard
1 photograph
Scissors
Glue

Gift-wrapping paper
Markers
Satin ribbon
Cello tape

Here we go
1. Cut the cardboard to the desired shape and size of the frame.
2. Stick the gift-wrapping paper on the cardboard. Allow to dry.

3. Now draw an outline of your photo on the back of the cardboard as shown.
4. With the help of an adult, cut inside the outline.
5. Stick the picture at the back using cello tape on all four sides.
6. Punch a hole near the top of the frame. String a satin ribbon through it.
7. You can decorate the frame with sequins, lace, trinkets and artificial stones. Hang it up on your favourite wall for all to see!

More to do

- To make a stand up frame, cut a rectangular cardboard strip the same size as the photoframe and stick it to the back of the photo. The photograph will actually be sandwiched between the two cardboard shapes. Bend the stand to such an angle that the frame can stand at a slant.
- You need not put only your photos in frames. You can frame your artwork and even pictures of your favourite cartoon characters.

Memory Cards

Here's a simple game that you can take wherever you go. Perfect for car trips, you can play it with a friend, sibling or even by yourself!

You will need
Cardboard
Scissors
Stickers/Pictures
White chart paper
Crayons/Markers

Here we go
1. Take a sheet of cardboard and stick white chart paper on it. Allow to dry.

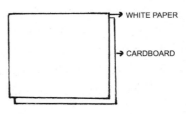

2. Cut up the cardboard into 40 squares or more of 1.5" x 1.5". The number of squares should be an even number.
3. Divide the squares into groups of two. Draw or stick pictures on each of the pairs. The only rule here is that every pair of cards must have the same picture.

4. Your game is ready, once you are done drawing!

How to play
1. Shuffle the cards and lay them face down.
2. Turn over two cards at random. If the two pictures match, the two cards become yours. If the pictures don't match, turn the cards over once again after memorising the pictures you saw on them so that the next time you find one of the pairs you will be able to tell what the other pair is.
3. Keep turning over the cards and matching the pictures.

It's more fun when you play this game with friends. So when they turn over their cards, you can observe what they have turned over and pick the right pair of cards the next time! The one with the largest number of pairs wins the game.

More to do
- Use a poster board instead of cardboard to make the cards. As the poster board is white on one side you can skip step 1.
- Make thematic memory cards with pictures of action heroes and their weapons or something informative like currencies and flags.

Greeting Card Curtain

MORE PAPER CRAFT

If you have a bunch of greeting cards saved over the years you can make a cool decoration for your room to hang up as a doorway curtain.

You will need
Old greeting cards   A compass
Fevicol
Satin ribbon (a little shorter than your doorway)
Cello tape   Scissors

Here we go
1. Choose 10 of your favourite greeting cards.
2. Using a compass, draw a circle of radius 1" on the back of the card.

3. Cut out the circle. Cut 10 such circles.
4. Place the circles on the satin ribbon equidistant from each other.
5. Stick the circles to the satin using Fevicol. Allow time to dry.
6. Make 5-6 such streamers or more depending on the width of the door.
7. After they are ready, attach the streamers to your doorway using cello tape.

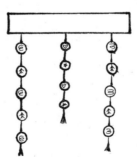

8. Your card curtain is ready! Add a touch of glitter glue to the ribbon to see a dazzling display.

More to do
- Make thematic curtains for different occasions. Make birthday decorative streamers with old birthday cards or a nice ornamental Christmas tree tinsel with old Christmas cards.
- You can cover your plain cupboards or windows with similar curtains made from cards. Try varying the lengths of the streamers for a cool effect!

Decoupage Box

Got some old cookie tins and chocolate boxes? Here is an easy way to revamp them and give them away as splendid gifts!

You will need

Old cookie tin
Water
Gift-wrapping paper

Cello tape
Scissors
Fevicol

Here we go
1. Stick a strip of cello tape along the rim of the box/tin.
2. Add 1 tablespoon of water to two tablespoons of Fevicol. Mix well and apply a layer on the tin.

3. Carefully place the gift-wrapping paper on the glue and wrap the bottom of the tin. Smooth out the wrinkles and creases. Your gift wrap must be below the strip of cello tape. Make sure that you choose the gift-wrapping paper according to what you would like to use the box for. So if it's going to hold hair accessories, you could get a pink gift wrap.

4. Coat the lid with the glue and stick the gift-wrap on the top. For the rim of the lid you can cut a strip of the gift-wrap and stick it around separately.

5. Now, using a flat paintbrush, paint the entire covered box with the glue. The glue will look whitish when applied but will turn completely transparent and shiny when dry.

6. Your decoupage box is ready to fill. And no one can ever guess that it was once an old cookie tin!

More to do
- Stick a bright satin ribbon on the rim of the lid instead of a strip of gift-wrapping paper for a brighter finish.
- You can decoupage the box using bits of coloured paper to get a collage-like effect.

Paper Earrings

MORE PAPER CRAFT

Have you ever heard of earrings made of paper? Here's how you can make them and what's more you can even pass them off as designer jewellery!

You will need
Colourful magazine paper
Toothpick   Fevikwik
2 earring wires (available in craft stores)
Scissors   Clear glitter nail polish (optional)

Here's how
1. Tear colourful pages from a magazine.
2. Cut them into 2" wide strips.
3. Fold the strips by bringing the ends to the centre. Press down well to smoothen the wrinkles.

4. Fold the strip again lengthwise in the centre.

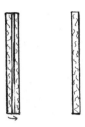

5. Now start rolling the strip into a tight coil from one end. Use a toothpick while rolling to get a tight coil.

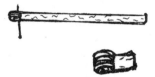

6. You can stick the coil bit by bit or just roll till the bottom and stick the end. Just make sure that the coil does not loosen or open up.
7. Place the coil on a flat surface and press down with the palm of your hand to flatten it.
8. Now, using a drop of Fevikwik, attach the wire to one side of the coil (the side that will be the back of the earring).

9. Your dangling earrings are ready! You can apply a coat of clear glitter nail polish all over the earrings for a shine. Wear them and watch your friends go ga-ga over them!

More to do

- Make a matching neck pendant and wear it around your neck. Just make a similar coil and attach a hoop at the back with Fevikwik. String a thread through the hoop and your neckwear is ready.
- If you want to hide the earring wire that will show at the back, simply stick another coil on top of the wire. In other words, your wire is to be sandwiched between two paper coils so that the ugly string cannot be seen! You will also have chunkier earrings this way.

Paper Jewels

Do you want some earrings and pendants that are shiny and smooth? All you need to do is make some shiny paper 3D jewels.

You will need
1 thin cardboard sheet   1 piece of sandpaper
Scissors   Fevicol
Clear glitter nail polish (optional)
Acrylic paints in metallic colours

Here we go
1. Decide the shape you want your jewel to be. Oval works best.
2. Draw the shape on a piece of cardboard. Cut it out.

3. Using this template, draw and cut out four more ovals so that you have five ovals in all.
4. Stick the ovals one on top of the other using Fevicol.
5. Let the ovals dry. Once dry, take a piece of sandpaper and rub the edges so as to smoothen the oval and give it a neat and clean finish.
6. Paint the front and the back of the oval using metallic colours.
7. Apply a coat of clear glitter nail polish on the oval jewel for a shiny finish or leave it as it is for a matte look.
8. Your jewel is now ready for use. Make many such shapes and use them to adorn your craft projects or add them as embellishments by sticking them to the coil earrings that you made earlier.

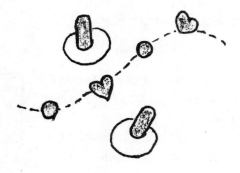

More to do
- For a different finish, use pearl acrylic colours. They will lend a nice shine to your jewel.
- Paint a border, add glitter and get creative with your jewel. You could even make a bag studded with them.

Paper Toffees

Have you ever been stuck in a situation where you needed to give a gift but couldn't go out to buy one? If you have an old cardboard tube, it won't take you long to make a cool, toffee-shaped gift for your friend.

You will need
1 paper tube of any length (toilet paper rolls, aluminium foil rolls, etc.)
1 metre thick satin ribbon
A small gift that fits into the tube
Some candy   Glitter
Cello tape
Shiny gift-wrapping paper (in gold or silver)

Here we go
1. Place the tube in the centre of the gift-wrapping paper. Leave enough space on all four sides to roll up the gift.

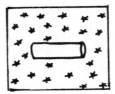

2. Fill the tube with stationery and candy or other such small items that you could gift your friend. Dust some glitter on to the tube.
3. Carefully roll the gift-wrap over the tube and secure it in place with cello tape.

4. Bunch up the loose ends of the paper on both sides and secure it with satin ribbons.
5. Your toffee is ready to give away.

More to do
- Paper toffees look great as party return gifts! Fill them with knickknacks, tiny toys, trinkets and balloons. Wrap the tube in keeping with the occasion or theme of the party.
- Stuff the ends of the tube with small strips or balls of gift-wrapping paper to keep your trinkets in place.

Hoops

If you want to give your room a festive look, you can make this streamer to hang up.

You will need
Old magazines   Scissors
Glue

Here we go
1. Cut 20 strips of paper of 6" x 1.5" from old magazines. Choose colourful parts of the magazine because the more colourful and glossier the paper, the better your streamer.
2. Stick the ends of one strip.

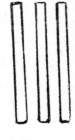

3. Now thread the second strip through the first and stick the ends once again.
4. Keep threading the strips as shown in the figure till all the strips are done.
5. Hang up your streamer from wall to wall with cello tape! Or simply suspend streamers of different lengths from a hook on your roof.

More to do
- Thread the last loop of the streamer through the first to get a paper chain that you can hang around your neck.
- Alternate the magazine strips with strips of gold and silver to adorn your house for a festive occasion!

Magnetic Notepad

How about making a personalised magnet notepad that you can stick on your refrigerator? It is fun and easy to make and extremely handy to jot down lists.

You will need
1 magnet sheet (available in craft stores)
White chart paper
Overhead Projection (OHP) sheet
Fevikwik   Scissors
Coloured cello tape (insulating tape)

Here we go
1. Cut a rectangle of size 6" x 3" from the magnet sheet.
2. Cut the chart paper and the OHP sheet to the same size.

3. Stick the white chart paper on the magnet sheet using Fevikwik.

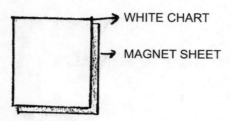

4. Now attach the OHP sheet to the chart paper and magnet sheet using cello tape on all sides.

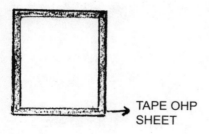

5. Put this on your refrigerator on the magnet side. With an OHP black marker, you can jot down all your lists in a jiffy! You can also erase it easily by using a sponge!

More to do
- Punch a hole on top of the notepad and attach your OHP marker to the notepad with a piece of satin ribbon.
- Add decorative stickers along the sides. Spell out the name of the person who will use the notepad using alphabet stickers on the top.

Shadow Box Display

MORE PAPER CRAFT

Do you have a lot of memorabilia lying around? How about displaying them on your wall? You will have a keepsake for life.

You will need
1 old shoebox
Dark coloured paper
Double-sided tape
OHP sheet/transparent paper
Memorabilia (friendship bands, feathers, ticket stubs, shells, etc.)

Scissors
Paper cutter
Cello tape

Here we go
1. Remove the lid of a shoebox and draw a rectangle on it as shown. There must be a 1" gap on all four sides of the rectangle.

2. With the help of an adult, cut out the rectangle neatly using a paper cutter. You will now have a rectangular hole in your lid.
3. Cut a rectangular piece from the OHP sheet that is just slightly larger than the hole.
4. Stick the OHP sheet to the inner side of the lid using transparent cello tape.
5. Now it's time to fill the box! You can stick dark coloured paper to the inside of your shoebox for an effective background.
6. Arrange your memorabilia attractively inside the box and stick them to the box using double-sided tape.
7. Now place the lid on the box and fasten it in place with cello tape.
8. Decorate the border of the lid using glitter and other embellishments.

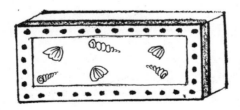

9. Your shadow box is ready for display! Perch it up on your shelf for all to see.

More to do
- You can also display other collections this way—coins, cards, shells or leaves—shadow boxes are a great way to display as well as protect your collections from getting tarnished.
- Shadow boxes make great frames for pictures, too. You can also carry your science projects to school in them.

Handprint Paper Stationery

How about making personalised stationery? All you need is your hand!

You will need
10 medium-sized white envelopes
Any dark coloured paint   A4 size paper

Here we go
1. Using a paintbrush, paint your left hand with a coat of black, dark blue or red paint.
2. Place your hand on the A4 sheet and carefully press down on the centre of the paper or on one of the corners.

3. Allow to dry.
4. Now go to a photocopy store and make 10 copies in black and white or in colour. Though colour photocopies look great, they might be a little expensive.
5. Also ask the photocopier to downsize your handprint picture and print it on envelopes.

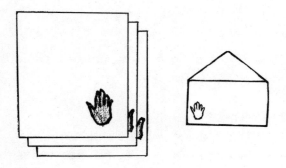

6. Gather up your sheets and envelopes and put them into a neat folder. Add a pen and you have your own personalised writing station sealed with your handprint!

More to do
- If you are making stationery for your friends, simply get their handprints on paper but don't reveal what's coming up! Surprise them with their own set of personalised stationery on their birthdays!
- Add your name or inspiring quotes in your best handwriting before taking the copies. You could also make stationery for your family with all your handprints overlapping each other. It would be perfect to send festival greetings on to friends and relatives.

Cut-out Cards

MORE PAPER CRAFT

Here's a greeting card with a difference. This one will not only sharpen your cutting skills but it will also look unique.

You will need

Tracing paper 1 white thick chart paper
Black carbon sheet 1 coloured paper
Paper cutter Glue
Scissor Pencil/Sketch pen

Here we go
1. Trace a picture of your choice using tracing paper as shown.

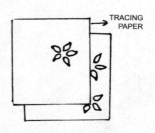

2. Cut the chart paper to the size of the picture. Fold the card in two.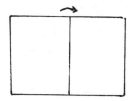
3. Transfer the picture on your tracing sheet onto the coloured paper.
4. Using a paper cutter or sharp scissors cut out the design carefully. Save all the cut out pieces.

5. The left side of the chart paper piece should be covered by the stencilled coloured paper and the right side should be plain.
6. Stick the cut-outs on the right side of the card by arranging them in such a way that they match the gaps in the stencil on the left side, part by part.

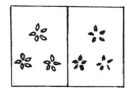

7. Your designer card is ready to be given away!

More to do
- The same thing can be done without folding the card in two. So you will have a cool picture that you can frame and hang!
- Choose designs that are easy to cut out for a start and then go on to complicated ones. This craft requires skill and patience, too!

Personalised Height Chart

How about a height chart that marks your growth? It can be an interesting addition to your room.

You will need
3 thick chart paper sheets of the same colour
Scissors   Black marker
Measuring tape   Cello tape
An assortment of photographs (from baby pictures to your current age)

Here we go
1. Cut the chart papers lengthwise in such a way that each strip is 1 foot in width.
2. Now arrange the strips on the floor one above the other in a line and measure the entire length using a

measuring tape. The length of the strips must not exceed 6 feet. If it does, remove or cut off the excess length.

3. With the help of an adult, tape the papers together. You should finally have a long strip of paper—1 foot wide and 6 feet long.
4. Leaving the strip on the floor, place a measuring tape along its side from bottom to top.
5. Carefully mark the inches on the left side of the paper starting from 0 till you reach the topmost point, approximately 72".
6. Mark the right side of the paper in feet from 0 to 6 in a similar manner.
7. Next mark your current height on the chart. Write down the date neatly in small print, using a marker.
8. Finally, stick your photographs in the middle of the chart —starting from the baby pictures at the bottom to the latest ones, next to your current height.
9. Your chart is ready! Tape it to

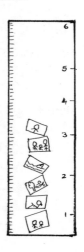

the wall using double-sided tape. Measure your height and jot it down on every birthday!

More to do
- Add more pictures as you increase in height. Overlap the pictures and add stickers or cut-outs to make the chart more colourful! If you can't find pictures, just draw a long coconut tree in the middle or the head of a giraffe with a long neck!
- Make a family height chart. Put an assortment of pictures of all the members along the middle and mark the height of each family member.

MORE PAPER CRAFT

Placemats

If you have a collection of pressed leaves and flowers, then this craft is just for you. For those of you who don't have a collection, start collecting.

You will need
Pressed leaves and flowers   Fevicol
Black Marker   Scissors
I thick white chart paper

Here we go
1. Cut a 12" x 16" rectangular piece from the chart paper.
2. Arrange the leaves and flowers on the chart paper in a decorative manner.

3. Add a tablespoon of water to two tablespoons of Fevicol. Mix well and apply carefully to the leaves and flowers before placing them on the chart paper.
4. Allow to dry.
5. Draw a decorative floral border with a black marker.
6. Finally take your paper to a laminating shop. Once laminated, you are done. You now have an easy wipe-clean placemat ready.

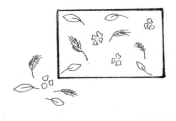

More to do
- Make an entire set for every place on your dining table. You could even make matching square coasters to complete the set.
- You need not stick to leaves and flowers alone, you could also use paper cut-outs or even a collage. All you need to do is laminate your creation after finishing so that it is firmly in place and stays forever.

Sun-prints

Here is a fun craft activity that you can do on a sunny summer day. Did you know that sunlight can bleach colours and make them fade? Try this activity to find out for yourself.

You will need
1 A4 size dark coloured paper
A heart shaped object (or any other shape)

Here we go
1. Place the object in the centre of the paper.
2. Put the paper out in the sun for a day with the object on top.

3. Remove the object in the evening and look at the paper. What do you see?
4. The place where you had placed the object will be darker than the rest of the paper. What's more, the shape of the object will be clearly defined! The sunlight has bleached the rest of the uncovered coloured paper to make it a couple of shades lighter! Make a card, a bookmark or cover your book with this sun-print paper!

More to do
- Try out different shapes and place many objects at a time. If you cannot find appropriate objects, cut out shapes from a cardboard sheet and place them on the paper with a stone on top for weight!
- If your paper doesn't get bleached, try keeping it out for a couple of days at noon. If it still remains the same, then the place where you live isn't hot enough!

Garden Mobile

How about a lightweight breezy mobile to hang in your garden or balcony?

You will need
Cardboard
Punching machine
Scissors
Green coloured paper
Thin wire
Coloured paper (at least 3 different colours for making flowers)

Here we go
1. Cut out a star shape from the cardboard. Your star should have six points. This will be the base for your mobile.
2. Punch holes on every point of the star as shown.

3. Cut out 3 flowers of different colours from the coloured paper. Punch a hole in the centre of each flower.

4. Cut out 3 leaves from the green paper. Punch a hole at the end of each leaf.
5. Measure and cut 6 wires of 12" each.
6. String the wires through the holes in the star.

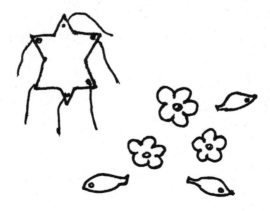

7. Thread one end of each wire through the holes in the flowers and leaves. Alternate the flowers and leaves for an attractive display.

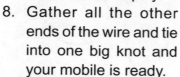

8. Gather all the other ends of the wire and tie into one big knot and your mobile is ready.
9. Suspend the mobile from a hook in the balcony or attach it to a tree in your garden for a delightful display.

More to do

- You can make layers by altering the length of the strings. You will have to punch more holes in the base star in that case.
- Paint the flowers, leaves and star with glow-in-the-dark paint. Your mobile will dance in the night as well!

Glass Painting

Did you know that you can simulate a glass painting with paper? Here's how.

You will need
Butter paper
Cello tape
Cellophane paper (of three colours–red, green, blue)
Paper cutter
Scissors
Glue stick

Here we go
1. Cut a 12" x 12" piece of butter paper.
2. Make a picture of a simple flower with six petals or any other motif you like.

3. Using a paper cutter carefully cut out the petals leaving behind the stencil framework of the flower. Keep the cut out petals carefully.

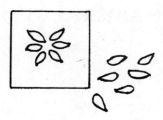

4. Place the petals on the cellophane papers and cut out the petal shape in all three colours. Cut a little extra around the petals so that you can stick them easily.

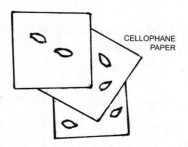

CELLOPHANE PAPER

5. Stick each petal to the back of the butter paper, exactly where the petals that have been cut out were, with a glue stick. Alternate the three colours while sticking.

6. Your fake glass art is done. Stick it to a glass window using cello tape and watch what happens when sunlight passes through the coloured cellophane.

More to do
- You can even measure your windowpane and cut the butter paper accordingly. After sticking the cellophane on the glass you can fasten the butter paper to your window with clear tape. You can cover all your windowpanes and pamper yourself with stained glass windows in your room!
- You can try the same technique to cover your switchboard as well! Alternatively, you can frame your painting and place it with your art collection!

Gift Toppers

Gift toppers are very easy to make and they come in handy for birthdays, weddings and other memorable occasions!

You will need
Old greeting cards   Thick chart paper
Punching machine   Small rubber band
Thin satin ribbons (three different colours)

Here we go
1. Cut attractive pictures from old greeting cards in any one of these shapes.
2. Cut the wording part of the card as well in any of the following shapes.

3. Cut a shape of your choice from the thick chart paper.
4. Now you will have three different shapes.
5. Punch holes on the top of each cut-out.
6. Cut three 6" pieces of satin ribbon of different colours. Thread the satin ribbons through the hole on top of the shapes.

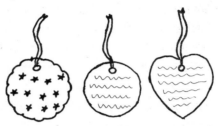

7. Place all three shapes together and braid the ribbons into a plait as shown. When you reach close to the end, tie a small rubber band to hold the braid in place.

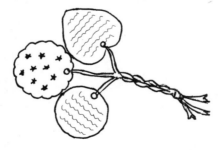

8. Your gift tag is ready. All you have to do now is stick or tie the gift tag to your wrapped gift.

Write your personal message in the blank shape that you cut out from the chart paper. Your message, along with the cut-outs from greeting cards, will make a sensational gift topper.

More to do
- Make a stock of these for different occasions. Cut out Christmas shapes like stars and bells for Christmas gift toppers. Birthday gift toppers can have the shape of a party hat or a cake!
- You could also follow the same procedure with just one cut-out. Thread the three coloured ribbons through the single hole and braid it the same way.

Drawer Divider

Are your drawers a constant mess with stationery, knickknacks and a lot of other junk? Make this handy drawer divider with a bunch of cardboard tubes.

You will need
4 or more cardboard tubes (from toilet paper rolls)
Fevibond
Gluestick
Gift-wrapping paper
Scissors

Here we go
1. Apply gluestick all over the tubes. Cut and stick gift-wrapping paper around each of the tubes as shown. The tubes should be of the same size.

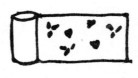

2. Arrange the paper tubes in any one of the following shapes.

3. Glue each of the tubes to the other using Fevibond.
4. Your drawer divider is ready. Empty your drawer and place this inside. Divide the contents of your drawer and categorise them. Place each category in a different hole. Your drawer will never be cluttered again.

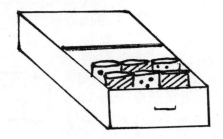

More to do
- Measure the size of your drawer and make the dividers accordingly from corner to corner. You can also stick the bottom of the dividers to a cardboard box and place the entire arrangement inside the drawer.
- Use the dividers for a fun game! Place the dividers on a table and play tossing the coin. Each of the tubes can have special points marked on the inside!

Cardboard Bulletin Board

If you want a place to display your to-do lists, photos and exam reminders, you can make this bulletin board.

You will need
2 sheets of corrugated cardboard (about 24" x 12")
½ metre printed cotton cloth (the size of the board)
Fevibond
Alphabet stickers
Satin ribbon
Pushpins/Thumbtacks

Here we go
1. Cut out two identical cardboard sheets of size 24" x 12".
2. Paste the two sheets one on top of the other using Fevibond.

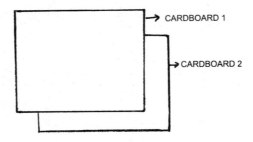

3. Allow to dry.
4. Stick the cloth on top of the cardboard sheet. Smoothen out the wrinkles and creases.

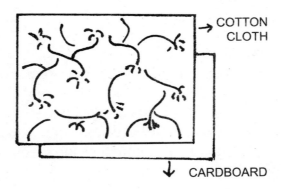

5. Spell out your name on the bulletin board using alphabet stickers. Use a little glue if the stickers do not stick easily on the cloth.

6. With the help of an adult, punch four holes on the board as shown.

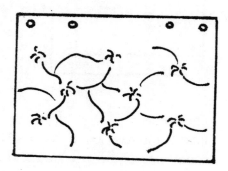

7. Thread a satin ribbon through the holes and hang up your bulletin board.

More to do
- Keep a supply of pushpins near the board. The pushpins will fasten and hold your reminders to the board.
- Make sure the covering cloth matches the décor of your house or the theme of your room. You can paint a border using fabric paints on the cloth.

Paper Quill Picture

Here's how you can do paper quilling without the use of special tools.

You will need
Toothpick   Glue
Coloured paper (any 1 colour)
Scissors   1 Cardboard piece

Here we go
1. Cut up the paper lengthwise into very thin strips—0.5 cm wide. The length of the strip should be at least 6".
2. Roll the paper strip over a toothpick so that it is a tight coil.

3. Stick the ends. Allow to dry.
4. Carefully remove the toothpick. You can even glue the inner coils so that they stay in place .
5. Make many such coils.
6. Place the coils close together or apart on a piece of cardboard to make pictures such as these.

7. Your quilling is complete. The circular coil is the first basic shape that one acquires while quilling. Check out books available on the same for making more complicated shapes!

More to do
- Before sticking the ends in step 3, allow the coil to naturally loosen a little. You will get loose coils instead of tight ones that look equally good.
- Pinch your coils in the corners to get other shapes like teardrops, ovals, triangles, etc. Get creative!

Tie and Dye Paper

You must have seen tie and dye t-shirts and other clothes. But what about tie and dye paper? Here's a fun way to make some really cool designer paper!

You will need
2 A4 white sheets
Paints
Spray bottle
Washable markers
Rubber band
Water

Here we go
1. Scrunch up one of the white papers into a ball.
2. Place the paper ball in the centre of another paper. Gather and tie up the ends with a rubber band.

3. Using markers, start at the bottom of the paper ball and make a colour filled circle as shown.
4. Add another concentric circle around this with a different colour.
5. Keep adding concentric circles of different colours. The circles can be of different sizes to produce different designs.
6. Finish off by adding colour to the scrunched up ends as well.
7. Fill a spray bottle with water.
8. Take the scrunched up paper to a balcony or garden and spray with water till the papers are wet and the colours seem to blend.

9. Allow the paper to sun dry.
10. Make sure the paper is completely dry before taking off the rubber band, otherwise the paper may tear.

11. Remove the rubber band and open up the two papers (this includes the one that was scrunched up as a ball).

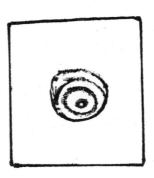

12. See the patterns the markers have made when blended. Smoothen out the wrinkles on the paper with the help of an adult, using a slightly warm iron.

More to do
- You can make all sorts of stuff with tie and dye paper. Gift-wrapping papers, greeting cards, bookmarks and craft projects—the list is endless.
- Don't use permanent markers as they do not blend together when sprayed with water. Always use a spray bottle for spraying the water. Direct sprinkling of water may lead to excessive soaking of the papers.

Waxed Paper Postcards

If you have lots of crayons stored away, bring out your cheese grater and have fun making this unique postcard!

You will need

Old wax crayons   Card paper/Thick chart paper
Butter paper   Grater
Towels/Dish rags   Iron

Here we go

1. Cut two rectangles of size 6" x 4" from butter paper.
2. Shred the wax crayons using a cheese grater into thin strips.
3. Place the wax strips evenly between the two sheets of butter paper.

4. Carefully place the paper sandwich between two towels.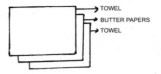
5. Iron the upper towel at low heat for two minutes.
6. Peek into the paper sandwich to check if the wax strips have melted.
7. Once the wax melts you will notice the colours merging and forming a lovely pattern!

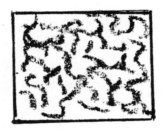

8. Remove the paper carefully and allow the wax to cool and harden.
9. Once it cools, stick it on to a piece of card paper of the same size to make a classy looking postcard!

More to do
- If the wax doesn't melt, increase the heat of the iron a little or iron for a while longer. Ask an adult to help you with the same.
- Care must be taken while handling hot wax as it can burn the skin badly.

Confetti

Throwing confetti at newly weds, at parties and celebrations is always fun! Here's an easy way to make confetti with some recycled paper.

You will need
An assortment of paper (coloured crepe paper, handmade paper, tissue paper, newspaper, etc.)
Shiny paper in gold, silver, red, green, etc.
Glitter   Scissors

Here we go
1. Cut up the different kinds of paper into little pieces. The trick to making confetti is to cut up the paper as finely as possible, so that people cannot make out easily what the confetti is made of!

2. Put the paper bits in a bowl.

3. Now cut up the shiny paper in a similar manner and add to the bowl.
4. Add three teaspoons of glitter powder to the bowl and mix thoroughly.
5. Your confetti is ready to sprinkle and throw!

More to do
- Add a handful of confetti to the inside of a greeting card before closing it. The recipient will get a pleasant confetti shower when he/she opens the card!
- Confetti can be used as a filler when you pack gifts. It can also be packed into balloons! Add a small pouch of confetti to your party return gift bags for extra fun.

Paper Blocks for 3D Origami

If you enjoy building blocks, you can make some paper blocks and have fun with them too.

You will need
White paper

Here we go
1. Take a small rectangular paper of size 7 cm x 5 cm.
2. Fold the rectangle into half as shown.

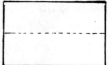

3. Now fold the rectangle once again into half and crease the paper well. Open the fold.

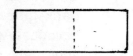

Note: All the folds are indicated with dotted lines.

4. Bring the upper corners of the paper towards the centre to make triangles as shown.

5. Turn the paper over and fold the bottom corners towards the base line of the triangle.

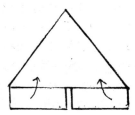

6. Fold the edges completely into the triangle as shown.

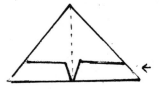

7. Now fold this into half along the centre crease that you had made in step 2. Your first paper block is ready!

8. Paper blocks are very simple to make. Once you have at least a 100 of them, you can make marvellous 3D creations as seen in the next activity.

More to do
- A4 paper works best for making the blocks. Instead of measuring and cutting up each paper, you can fold the A4 paper four times to get 16 rectangles. Cut up the rectangles and fold each of them into individual paper blocks as instructed above.
- Try using coloured sheets as well. Make a set of blocks with three or more colours to help you mix, match and make!

Origami Wreath

Now that you have some paper blocks ready you can make a simple 3D wreath. The paper blocks contain two pockets and two tails. These pockets and tails are the key to holding your origami shapes together.

You will need
100 paper blocks (made earlier)

Here we go
1. Place the first origami block on the table. Slip the tail of a second block into one of the pockets of the first one.

2. Tighten the link so that the blocks do not slip.

3. Keep adding blocks the same way till you get a long string of blocks.

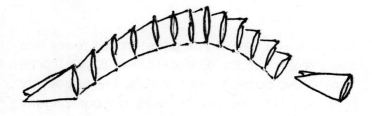

4. When you have linked at least 50 blocks this way, slip the tail of the first block into the pocket of the last to make a circle.
5. Keep tightening the links as you go along, so that the tails of the blocks do not slip out of the pockets. Your paper wreath is ready with no glue, mess or fuss!

More to do
- Use coloured paper instead of plain white and make a rainbow-coloured wreath.
- In step 2 we added a block to only one pocket while the other pocket remained empty. Add a block to the empty pocket as well. Now your blocks will grow in steps. One block will lead to two blocks and two blocks will lead to four and four to eight and so on! In this way you can make umpteen 3D designs that simply grow!

Cake Toppers

MORE PAPER CRAFT

Do you run around at the last moment to find cake toppers and candles? Here's a fun paper mache craft that you can make with cardboard and old newspapers.

You will need

Cardboard   Newspaper
Scissors   Fevikwik
Fevicol   Birthday candles
Embellishments (stones, tiny flowers, etc)

Here we go
1. Cut out number shapes using cardboard.
2. Mix Fevicol with an equal amount of water in a bowl.

3. Tear newspaper strips and keep them separately.

4. Coat the cardboard number with the Fevicol mixture, using a brush.
5. Wrap the newspaper strips over the glue in a random manner.
6. Apply glue to the first layer of strips and wrap another layer of newspaper strips on top of the first.
7. Keep applying glue and wrapping till your creation starts getting a proper three-dimensional shape.
8. When the number shape appears bulky enough, stop wrapping and allow it to dry completely.
9. Paint the number with acrylic paints.
10. Using a sharp pencil, make small holes along the number. The number and the holes must be equal. For example, if you have made the number 2, you must make two holes only.

11. Using a drop of Fevikwik, attach thin birthday candles to the holes.
12. Add embellishments along the number wherever you find empty spaces and impress your friends at your birthday party.

More to do
- Make a set with all the numbers from 0 to 9. You can mix and match the numbers for a long time!
- Give this cake topper as a gift. You can mould any shape the same way by cutting the cardboard to that particular shape. You can also embellish the shape before gifting it.

Art Corner

Love to draw on walls? Then make your very own art corner where you can draw, scribble, doodle and paint without damaging your house!

You will need
4 thick chart paper sheets of the same colour
An empty wall   Transparent cello tape
Coloured cello tape

Here we go
1. Arrange the four chart papers on the floor.

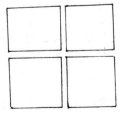

2. Tape them to each other in the centre using coloured cello tape.

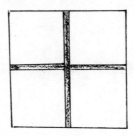

3. Make a border along all the four edges using the same tape. The cello tape must be stuck along the border completely.
4. Now with the help of an adult, stick this drawing board on an empty wall using transparent cello tape.
5. The base is ready. You can decorate the top of the drawing board with some origami artwork such as paper boats, paper kites and so on. Now you can start doodling.

More to do
- If you have filled the drawing board with your sketches, gently remove it from the wall without peeling the paint and replace it with another one. Or you can stick a new drawing board neatly on top of the old one.
- You can give a cardboard backing to the chart paper drawing board and hang it on a nail instead of sticking it on the wall.

Pocketbook

MORE PAPER CRAFT

Paper books are very simple to make and they can hold lots of information! Here's a cute accordion style pocketbook that you can make easily.

You will need

Chart paper   2 small cardboard pieces
Scissors   Gift-wrapping paper
Decorative items (stickers, stones, sequins, etc.)
Glue

Here we go
1. Cut out a 5" wide strip of chart paper lengthwise.
2. Fan fold the paper strip accordion style (like a paper fan) so that each fold is at least 2" in width. Fold the creases neatly.

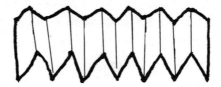

3. Cut off the excess paper from the ends.
4. Open up the paper strip and place it on a table.
5. Cut two cardboard pieces of size 5" x 2".
6. Cover the cardboard pieces with gift-wrapping paper.
7. Stick the cardboard pieces on the first and the last fold of the accordion on the same side.

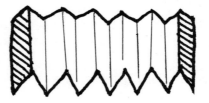

8. Fold the paper once again along the creases and press well such that the two cardboard pieces form the front and back covers of your book.

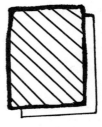

9. Decorate the front cover and you can fill your pocket book with lists, phone numbers, addresses and even secrets!

More to do
- You can make the above book in any size provided the book is rectangular in shape. Bigger books can be used for scrap booking!
- If you want your book to hold a lot more pages, simply attach one paper strip to the other by overlapping the papers with a little glue. Now your book will be really long! But don't make it too long! If you do, it will be difficult to shut and it will open up like a spring!

Venetian Mask

Venetian masks are different from ordinary paper masks. Venetian masks have weird mystic shapes that make them unique.

You will need
2 paper doilies   Thick chart paper (any colour)
Glue   Silver glitter
Scissors   Unsharpened new pencil
Embellishments (small stones, lace, etc)
Fevicol

Here we go
1. Stick a paper doily on a piece of chart paper.

2. Now cut out the shape as marked in the figure.
3. Place the mask on your face and carefully mark the eye holes with a pencil at the back.

4. Cut out the eye holes carefully without damaging the doily lace.

5. Take another paper doily and cut it into four quarters.
6. Stick one of the quarters at the back of the mask.
7. Next coat a pencil with Fevicol.
8. Place it on a sheet of newspaper and sprinkle glitter all over it. Allow the pencil to dry thoroughly.
9. Attach the pencil to the back of your mask.

10. Decorate your mask with a few glittering embellishments, preferably small stones or lace. Do not overdo it or the elegance of the mask will be lost. Hold the mask close to your face for a carnival look!

More to do
- You can use long flower-making pipe strands that you can get in craft stores instead of a pencil.
- Make three such masks with chart papers of different shades to make a stunning wall display.

Point-a-Picture

MORE PAPER CRAFT

Here is a fun project that will keep you engaged for hours.

You will need
Chart paper
Pencil
Scissors
Thermocol sheet
Board pin
Double-sided tape

Here we go
1. Cut a 7" x 7" square from the chart paper.
2. Draw the shape of a butterfly on the chart paper.

3. Place the chart paper on the thermocol sheet.
4. Using a board pin poke holes at equal distances, all along the outline of the butterfly.

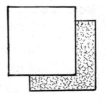

5. Detail the inside pattern of the butterfly in a similar manner.

6. Once you have made holes all along the shape (outline as well as inside), trim the chart paper to the shape of a butterfly.
7. Hang it up on a sunny glass pane and watch the light come through the holes.

More to do
- Try this with papers of different colours and with different designs. You could outline a bat on black paper or a bunch of hearts on red paper for some dramatic results.
- Instead of putting the design on a windowpane, stick a paper of a contrasting colour at the back. For example, if you have stencilled on black paper, you can stick white paper at the back. The colour at the back will show through. This can also make a good greeting card.